QUE is comforting and has brought me home to myself and to the power I have within. - Leah Scott

QUE is coming back home within...connecting mind, body, soul into a container of flow and expansion. - Martha Catherine Wahl

QUE is where I find me. When I'm feeling off or out of sorts I close my eyes, connect in with my heart and remind myself...I've got the power. - Christine Roy

QUE is like an ancient future filled with potential medicine. It unlocked the bigger part of me that forgot about its creative forces that are already within me but needed to be activated and nourished. - Edyta Cote

In a world of perception, QUE is my TRUTH. When I am lost, looking or misaligned, it is the purest flow of creation that brings me back to my eternal home. - Mocha Butkovitch

QUEing Up Magic

How to Have What You Want When You Want it Through Advanced Manifestation

Joy Kingsborough

STOKE Publishing

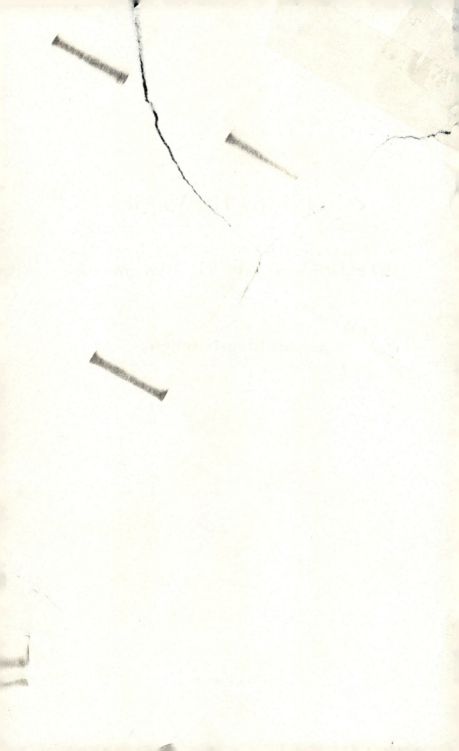

How to Have What You Want When You Want it
Through Advanced Manifestation

QUEing Up Magic

Joy Kingsborough

QUEing Up Magic
Copyright © JoyKingsborough 2023.
ISBN: 978-1-7388246-1-8

Interior Design by STOKE Publishing
Author photo credit: Monika Broz Photography

All rights reserved. No part of this publication may be reproduced, stored in a retrieval system, or transmitted, in any form or by any means, without prior written permission of the author, Joy Kingsborough.

Contents

You Are UniQUE
1. The Body-Mind   5
2. The Observer-Mind   7
3. The Essential-Mind   9

The QUEst for Awakening
4. The PreQUEL   17
5. The SeQUEL   21
6. The ThreeQUEL   29

What is QUE?   37

Taking the "Woo" Out of Manifestation
7. The Divine Timing Cycle of Manifestation   49
8. The Universe is Neutral   61

The Essential FreQUEncies
9. The Essential FreQUEncies   69
10. YOUniversal Awakening   73

Advanced Manifestation
11. Taking the Leap   81

About the Author   85
Are You Looking For A Speaker?   87

A special thank you to all of the students of MindSHIFT who have helped ripple the impact of QUE into the world.

You Are UniQUE

"The ALL is Mind. The Universe is mental." – The Kybalion

You have likely heard the phrase; you are a spiritual being having a human experience. This phrase implies that you are separate from your human experience. However, this is not true. You are one with the human and the spirit and the mind – you are a 3-part energy body I call a YOUniverse. You are the very essence of life, experiencing itself from different points of view.

Authors have written about the true nature of who we are for eons, always offering the caveat that what we are is beyond words and is something that must be experienced to be understood. I wholeheartedly agree. Yet, I will attempt, in this book, to offer some words that may help point you in the direction of your whole self and I hope it will inspire you to have a direct experience.

To have an experience of your whole self is the reason for this book and the mission behind my work with Quantum Expansion or QUE. This practice is simple, offering a predictable and repeatable path to a direct experience of yourself in an ongoing, persistent state. That means the practice of QUE helps you express yourself as the fullest version, not just sometimes, but all the time. QUE opens you to the benefits of persistent wellbeing, wealth, love, and connection.

Before I tell you more about QUE, I must tell you about YOU.

In my personal and professional experience, working with thousands of individuals over the last 20 years, I have witnessed 3 unique, but interconnected, aspects of the whole self that operates as 3 levels of body. These 3 body levels are contained by a field of energy, each with a mind that works together as the whole self. You can consider yourself a monad – or contained, organized mind.

You are not, only, the body you live in or the thoughts you think or the feelings you feel. You are a multidimensional being who is traveling with and within the physical body. The thoughts you think, the decisions you make, and the desires you have are all happening outside of your physical body in 2 expanded dimensional body states. You are influenced by these other dimensions whether you are aware or not. The more aware you are about these other dimensions, the more leverage you have.

You manifest experience at the physical body level which tricks you into believing that this is the only place that you exist. Remembering that you are so much more than a physical body and learning to work with all 3 bodies (physical and multi-dimensional) is where you have the most power and influence to create your reality.

1. **The Physical Body or Body-Mind (Body)**
2. **The Emotional Body or Observer-Mind (Observer)**
3. **The Essential Body or Essential-Mind (Essence)**

Chapter 1

The Body-Mind

The Body-Mind is the doer in the body that is physically focused.

The physical Body-Mind is made up of everything that is contained around the skeletal structure and beneath the skin. You have automatic processes at this level and respond to environmental conditions in accordance with mental (beliefs) and biological (dna) patterns.

The Body-Mind is focused on the survival of its structure in the material, 3rd-dimensional world in which it performs tasks (does things). The Body-Mind wants to live long enough to carry out its tasks. Fear, approval, pleasure and the avoidance of pain and death is the primary driver of behavior for the Body-Mind.

The Body-Mind is always building something and breaking something down. The body is self-repairing based on the pattern it is following. Repair is a body level function that will continue until the end of its time as this body. When it comes to its death date, the cells of the body will be returned to a state of pure energy and used in new ways. The rest of you will continue in new forms.

Chapter 2

The Observer-Mind

The Observer-Mind is the chooser that can be physically or spiritually focused.

The Observer-Mind directs the sensory system through the auric field to deliver messages (thoughts) to the body. The Observer-Mind chooses the pattern of thoughts the body has access to. The Observer-Mind is dependent on what it sees with its inner or outer perceptions to determine which patterns the body should use.

The Observer-Mind is responsible for choosing patterns for the physical body so that it can thrive, from a 4th-dimensional world view of time and space. Its primary directive is identifying patterns that are out of sync with desires by deleting them, editing them, or writing new ones. The Observer-Mind decides what the meanings of all events are for the body.

There are infinite possibilities to choose from, but the Observer-Mind must focus by filtering through discernment of right and wrong; good and bad; virtues, values, and preferences as well as beliefs about what is possible. This part of us has the power to re-write any pattern and to create any condition it deems possible. The process of altering patterns is called healing. When the Observer-Mind discovers a condition and chooses to change it, a new pattern enters the Body-Mind and behavioral change occurs. The body experiences the symptoms of healing in ways that are sometimes painful, uncomfortable, or messy depending on the pattern that is changed.

Chapter 3

The Essential-Mind

The Essential-Mind is the Seer who is holistically focused on your greater purpose.

The Essential-Mind is made up of a vibrational system that operates at the level of the Quantum Field. The Essence is focused on higher purpose and meaning, from a 5th-dimensional perspective of unity and love. The Essence experiences desire or resistance and is in a state of surrender to higher knowing, truth, and alignment with the Source (the One, God, Universe, etc.). The Essence is a direct bridge between higher dimensions and the rest of the self.

When you become aware of the Essence you unlock your wholeness and integrate as a single being, or YOUniverse, made up of all 3 parts of self. The Essence offers guidance and direction for the path ahead, based on the vibrational state of the YOUniverse and the world around you. The Essence is bound by the perspective of "now." The Essence is only focused in this moment and is responsible for guiding you to make the best decisions for the future from the current moment possibilities. The Essence is like having a Universal look out who can see further down the road, around the corners, and past any obstacles.

The Essence has no judgments, fears, or insecurities as this part of you moves at a dimensional frequency of the 5th dimension. In simple terms, the Essence can see that you are united as one with everything and everyone. The Essence does not experience separation and has no limits to love or expression. When the Essence, Observer, and Body-Mind work together they are a force majeure – irresistible and uncontrollable.

QUE will help you bring these parts of yourself together instantly.

When you bring these 3 aspects of self together the physical body is lit up, energized, and certain about what is next. The Essence can predict conditions and may offer visions, images, blueprints, or feelings about what the future might look like, but is focused on creating the conditions now one step at a time. This allows for shifts and changes along the way that better match what is unfolding as it is created in real-time (aka now).

The Essence has all available information in the form of vibrational awareness, which is why this is the most aligned and accurate information to go by. It is unique to you, based on the information available about the co-creation of the entire universe in each precise moment. This is how you tap into magic – listening to the Essence and trusting the guidance. When you act on the information it provides, despite the lack of evidence available to prove the outcome at the body-mind level, your life will expand in love, abundance, and joy!

You are a YOUniverse.

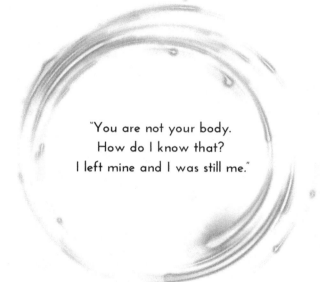

"You are not your body.
How do I know that?
I left mine and I was still me."

The QUEst for Awakening

My story began with tragedy. I suffered abuse, abandonment, loss, and poverty. I worked hard and struggled to survive every day and prayed for something or someone to change my life every night until I was 35. By the time I was in my 20s I had come to believe that tragedy was a way of life. My motto back then was, "to have a little sunshine, one must endure the rain." Endure is what I excelled at.

When I was 27, I met Terry, the greatest love of my life. I believed my prayers had been answered when we fell in love. Except, I didn't believe that prayers could last. Dreams didn't come true for me, at least not for long. As soon as Terry proposed I knew the rain would be coming soon.

Terry was full of life and was so eager to shower me with love. His adoration and devotion were something out of a fairytale. I wasn't struggling anymore, and I felt happier than I had in my entire life. I began to believe that love was for me, and my life was going to be okay after all. I allowed myself to fantasize about the future and make plans for a life together.

As predicted, the rain arrived, and it turned out to be a hurricane. Six months before we were to be married Terry was diagnosed with terminal Cancer. He died within months. We never walked down the aisle. As fast as love had come into my life it was ripped away.

Before Terry's death I believed in God. I had explored churches and various belief systems hoping to understand God more personally. I wanted to understand why life was so difficult and how I could do better or be better to have a better life. After Terry died, my beliefs about God shifted dramatically. I no longer experience God as a personified, religious deity. I experience God as everything, everywhere, in all things and people at once. God is an energy. I do not call this energy God; I call it the Source.

The Source is an all-encompassing word for me that considers all possible interpretations at once. There is a Source, organizing intelligence that has somehow, someway, created this world we live in. I no longer need to know what the right word use is, or the right description. Source cannot be fully described. Nor do I have any desire for anyone to believe what I believe or call God by the same name.

Your belief systems around human origins, God, or religion have no bearing on your ability to use the techniques in this book. Nothing I am sharing in this book is intended to take away from your belief systems or personal experiences with God. I honor you as I honor myself. Somehow all our ideas belong. At any time, if you feel uncomfortable with a word I choose to use, please replace it in your mind with one of your own.

If you have no belief in a Source or creator that is okay too. If you are open and curious and willing to play with the well-documented reality that intelligence and energy is all there is, you can benefit from the practices in this book immensely. We may never collectively agree about the origins of humanity, but we can learn to live together in more harmony, collaboratively with nature and each other.

The techniques I express and the ideas I share about your true essence need not conflict with religion; however, it may challenge some of your beliefs about reality. If that occurs, remember to take what works for you and leave the rest. The goal of this book is not to convince anyone that the Source is or is not real. Your understanding of energy (Source, Universe or God) is something you must experience for yourself. The Source is real for me but how I perceive the Source may not be the way it looks or feels for you. Just as gravity works for all of us, so too will QUE work for you.

Ultimately, we are powerful co-creators that have the innate ability to influence our future individually and collectively by accepting that there is more to reality than physical constructs. That is the core message of this book.

Chapter 4

The PreQUEL

You are not your body. How do I know that? I left mine and I was still me.

Hundreds of thousands of people all around the world have experienced near death experiences (NDE) or out of body experiences (OBE). I am one of those people. When Terry died, I felt lost and alone. I wanted to be with Terry wherever he was. I believed my life was over and I would never find happiness without him. So, one night I drank myself unconscious, hoping to die.

I emerged out of my body into a stream of light, floating through the Universe in an infinite stream of energy that looked like stars. I knew without being told that I was leaving the 3rd dimension and was no longer my human self. For a time, I didn't remember my name or what had happened to me before this moment, I just enjoyed being in the loving embrace of this stream of light. Peace and love were present with me as was my ability to think and observe what was happening.

There were no emotions present, only the ability to observe. The longer I traveled in this stream of consciousness, the more I began to know about life. I remembered that I had chosen to be alive before I was born into the last body. I remembered that I didn't do what I set out to do. I had gone through the most difficult part and was now on my way to fulfilling my purpose. If I didn't go back soon, I would be reborn into a new body and must do the hard part again. I wanted to go back. The pull to return to my body became strong, like a magnetic force that brought me back to the body in an instant.

I could feel myself returning to the body. The body felt intense pressure as I returned through my chest. It felt as though I had fallen back inside through what felt like a small hole in the heart and all the emotions returned at once. I replayed the events in my mind but could only remember a handful of details. There were other things I learned and experienced that the body couldn't comprehend at the time, but I slowly integrated in the years that followed.

What was I when I was out of the body?

Coming back to the body I live in; I could not shake the experience that there is so much more to who we are as humans. I was having a real experience outside of the body. I was accessing wisdom that was beyond space and time. I was accessing a plan that was bigger than the body-mind could comprehend. Yet, I could also feel a love for life that was so expansive, so consuming that it changed my relationship to life forever. It's been 20 years since my out of body experience and I still wake up every day and choose to love my life.

I came back knowing that the quality of the body you were born into does not make you any more or less you. Whether you have arms and legs, full or limited mobility, your body does not stop you from being the expression of your true self. You are and will always be whole in any form you take.

I came back knowing that the power that flows through each of us holds limitless potential. You are the energy that animates the body. Without you, your body cannot live. With you, your body becomes more healthy and vital.

I came back knowing that everything we want to have in the material, 3-dimensional world, is ultimately already within us.

When the body becomes aware of you at this higher level it awakens and begins the journey of ascension to a higher dimensional experience of self. This higher dimensional experience of self includes the physical and emotional aspects as well as the non-physical, timeless aspect as one being, merged and operating from its higher awareness of reality. Your life becomes magical.

As already stated, I call the non-physical, timeless part of ourselves the Essence, the emotional self the Observer, and the physical self the Body-Mind. This triune of selves forms a monad; one conscious Mind. Each is equal in importance, limited in its individual focus, and limitless when harmonized or merged.

The Essence is the part of you that animates the body and chooses to come to Earth. The Essence is the part of you aware of your purpose and the bigger reasons for your life. Before I left my body, I was not aware of the

Essence or the Observer. I was living life from the perspective of the Body-Mind, and I was trapped in fear, loneliness, and feelings of unworthiness.

When I came back to the body, I felt loved, and connected, and my life had meaning. I didn't know how the experience would change my life; I just knew it would never be the same again.

Chapter 5

The SeQUEL

After my out-of-body experience in 1999 I became an active seeker of information that could help me understand what had happened to me and what it meant. I wanted to understand the nature of the world, the meaning of life, and the nature of death, birth, and rebirth. I was having an existential crisis and awakening.

I had already been experiencing unexplainable phenomena, like seeing what I thought were ghosts or energy beings, feeling presence around me, and persistent flickering of my home's lighting. I was feeling other people's emotions and could perceive events before they would happen, and I was hearing a voice coming into my mind from just above me, that I believed was a spirit guide of some sort. The voice was kind and loving and always invited me to take responsibility, to make better decisions, and to love myself more.

My out of body experience had opened my higher senses and I wasn't sure what to make of anything I was seeing or feeling. Was I experiencing a mental disorder, having a breakdown, or having a true spiritual experience? I sought the support of various mentors to help me piece together what was happening. I remember being guided to sense the energy moving between my hands by a mentor. She was helping me see and feel the energy that was around me and inside of me. She was pointing me to my Observer by helping me see where my body ended and the rest of me began. She was helping my Body-Mind awaken.

My Body-Mind was blown away by how it could direct a thought to have an experience and then I would have the experience. I thought about the energy moving between my hands, rubbed them together for a few moments and then pulled them apart to feel the sensation of the heat and friction between my hands. It was an exercise that was repeatable and predictable.

I wanted to understand how that exercise worked. Over the next 10 years I explored various teachings, training, and a graduate program in psychology. I discovered Bruce Lipton, Anna Weiss, Candice Pert and other academics, and scientists who were studying biology and neuro-phenomena to help me understand at a cellular level how the body responded to various experiences.

This led me to meditation.

I was introduced to a form of meditation through a friend who had experienced a similar awakening to energy and the vast unseen world around us. He helped me understand that meditation is not simply about quieting the mind or resting in silence, it is a body-state change that opens you up to limitless mental, emotional, and physical experiences. Through that process I was able to witness my body as a mind in observation of it, unidentified with the body. I experienced myself as something more, something beyond the material part of me. I reached the state of being that I had felt years before, as a young woman grieving the loss Terry, in my out of body experience.

I was in the quantum field, and I was connecting with a state of Oneness that I called Source. Others have called this energy God, the One, Source, the Universe and so on. In this simple practice, I discovered a predictable, repeatable pathway to Source. I could connect, communicate, and experience the love and comfort of Source anytime I wanted.

Over the next 10 years I would immerse myself in this amazing practice, meditating for many hours every day. I would go on to teach meditation and explore other ways of connecting with the Source through ceremony, shamanistic practices, and divining. The anxiety in my body disappeared, I lived in a profound state of peace, and my desire to help others became dominant. My life was profoundly changed during that time as I learned to witness my life in new ways. I was less interested in my challenges and more interested in how I could create my reality.

Becoming more aware through meditation opened the door to the next stage of awakening, facing my shadow and turning my life over to the Observer.

Once my Observer expanded its awareness of what was possible through meditation, the healing journey began. I woke up one morning crying uncontrollably for no obvious reason. I was sad, angry, and disappointed by my past. Before my awakening I had been consumed in drama, suffering, and abuse. Now, I love my life and have been blessed in so many ways. I had so much to give, but felt immense shame, blame and guilt for not awakening sooner. My past needed to integrate with my current experience which meant my patterns needed to change. I needed to heal.

I shared my feelings with my family and proposed an adventure. We agreed to sell everything and move to a remote location where I could write, cook, raise the kids, and meditate in nature. So, my husband, and 2 children and I spent nearly a year in virtual isolation from the world. We spent our days surrounded by a forest filled with animal life, a spectacular mountain, and a lake just a few steps from our front door. At night we talked by the fire and gazed at the stars. This lifestyle had granted me the time to immerse myself in hours-long meditations each day where I was having profound experiences with Source and nature.

Slowly, gently, I was guided by Source to love and forgive myself for the past, facing the emotions that had been buried deep inside of me. I reconciled who I was with who I had become. I accepted that I was a spirit and a body and had limitless potential. As I healed, I saw my life with more clarity. I wanted to help others heal themselves too, but I didn't want to face the world or the changes that I knew I needed to make.

I didn't want to lose the peace and comfort of the little bubble I was living in. It would be noisy back in the city and I didn't know if I was ready or if I ever wanted to go back. There was so much love available when I meditated, that I just wanted to escape into the safety and warmth of Source every chance I got. I was living a dream life and finally felt like I needed no one, or nothing outside of myself to make me happy.

One afternoon, I was by myself meditating on a chair just a few feet from the water having a familiar experience of oneness. I had been there for many hours and was now feeling one with the land and the animals. No longer a threat, the wildlife around me came alive, embracing my presence. I could hear a beaver gathering sticks to reinforce its home just a few feet away. Birds were all around and the water was still, like glass.

I felt as though I was living in a painting; it was pure magic. I could feel the connection between all that is. The energy that I felt between my hands those years ago was now radiating above every inch of my body, I could see the energy waves in colors of blue, purple, and yellow. The energy beaming back and forth between me and the mountains, the lake, the animals, connecting us as one. I wanted to stay at that lake forever and never see the world of humans again. I could have easily slipped into the life of a hermit and been incredibly content.

Life had other plans for me. It was time to go.

As I gazed out at the lake I witnessed a bald eagle dive down from the sky, shattering the glass lake, plucking a salmon out of the water with its talons. He paused, clutching the salmon, and hovered above the water for just a moment, staring at me. We were eye level with one another and about 100 feet apart. I was mesmerized by his presence and his strength. During those few seconds I heard a whisper from Source, "you have nourished yourself with this land and this time, but you are complete. It's time to bring back what you have learned and live it, so that you can share it with the world." Then, the eagle, with fish in tow, flew away.

I got up from my chair and began packing to move.

Within a few weeks my family and I returned to civilization. Naively, I began looking for ways I could help others, completely ignoring the most important part of the message. I would need to live what I learned. That was my first big lesson in awakening. To awaken is profound, but to put what you discover into practice is the only way to experience transformation or ascension to a new life.

Leaving my idyllic life on that lake would open the door for 7 more years of healing the sadness, disappointment, and betrayal that I had no idea was lurking in even deeper parts of myself. I needed support for this part of the journey, which led me to Reiki where I would unlock an even deeper connection to Source than I had experienced before.

Reiki, if you are not familiar with it, is a healing modality that teaches practitioners to guide the loving energy of the universe through the physical body of both the practitioner and the client for the purposes of healing and restoring wholeness. I fell in love with this modality and was certified as a master/teacher as quickly as possible. I applied the techniques I learned to heal my pets, family, and anyone who would let me practice. I launched a healing practice teaching meditation, consulting on nutrition, and offering reiki sessions.

The more I worked with clients the more I discovered my own pain and trauma was rising up to be healed. I would perform a session with a client and then a session for myself. It was an amazing experience of loving and embracing myself through the gentle nurturing of what healers call our shadow. Our shadow is part of our Body-Mind where we hold our judgements, shame and trauma so that we can protect ourselves from having to deal with them. The shadow holds the parts of ourselves that we want to keep from others, that we feel ashamed of, and fear others would not accept us if they knew about them.

NOTE:

We all have a shadow where we hide these parts. The shadow is not inherently a problem, it is the denial of the shadow or the unwillingness to take inventory of what lives there that can create problems in our life. Many of you reading this will be familiar with the shadow and have likely done the work to face these parts of yourself. If you haven't, I highly recommend working with someone to uncover these aspects, as that will make the manifestation process easier and faster. You can choose to proceed without doing this work with someone else, but you will need to have immense patience and kindness with yourself.

If you aren't new to the shadow and have experience healing as a practitioner or a client, you will find the process of QUE will help you release any remnants of past influences rapidly. While QUE is not a healing technique, it will create a cleanse response in the body at the physical, emotional, and vibrational level. We will talk more about that later.

During those years I discovered what it meant to live what I had learned in my awakening. I learned to surrender to life, to let go of the past and to believe in a better future. My day-to-day life improved and the peace, ease, and freedom I felt in my body was something I never dreamed possible. With Reiki, I faced the shame, felt the anger, and cried – a lot! I felt years younger, pounds lighter, and my faith was renewed.

I thought my story would end there. I was so happy and helped so many people. At the same time there were some key areas in my life that still needed to change. I just couldn't figure out how to make those changes without a lot of effort and struggle and I knew there was an easier way. Everything up to this point had shown me that the Universe is simple, and awareness is everything. Clearly, there was something I didn't know I just couldn't put my finger on what it was. I was being pointed to my Essence.

Chapter 6

The ThreeQUEL

I have always wanted to know Source. I think we all long to be seen and loved and approved of. We want to understand why we were born and if our life matters. I will never forget that first time I felt an other-worldly presence. I was 5 years old and attending a church service. I felt a strong emotion and strange sensation in my head, heart, and belly. It felt like the cells in my body were leaping forward, urging me to leave my seat. I would normally be afraid to leave my Mom's side, but I was overwhelmed by something that seemed bigger than me, bigger than my Mom, and even bigger than the room itself. I got up and walked to the front of the service where I saw other people praying at the foot of the altar. I joined them. I wanted to be a part of that energy. I wanted to feel more of it. I didn't want it to stop. I wanted to feel that energy within me forever.

Of course, the music eventually stopped, and we all went back to our seats. The sermon began and I soon lost the feeling in my body, but it had been imprinted in my heart forever. I would never forget that moment, but I wouldn't find it again until a meditation in Boulder, Colorado shortly after Terry's death.

I was invited to a women's circle for a guided meditation to meet our Spirit Guides. I relaxed onto my blanket on the floor and listened to the amazing, guided voice inviting me to relax my body and open my heart and mind to the unknown. That was the night I met Jonah.

The last thing I remember hearing was, "Someone has come to meet you, welcome them now and ask for their name…." the meditation guide's voice began to trail off in the distance as an image entered my mind. I saw a slender, 7-foot-tall man in a vibrant, very flamboyant genie costume. He wore bright purple and blue and yellow metallic polyester that shimmered with every movement of his body. His outfit was over the top, but beautiful. I immediately giggled and felt safe.

I asked for his name, and he said, "Jonah." I was hearing all of this through my inner ears and seeing it all with my inner eyes, but it was as real as anything I have ever experienced. He continued speaking, "dance with me!" I felt myself get up even though my body lay still on the floor, and I danced with him. We danced and laughed, and I felt at home. I felt as though I had known him forever, many lifetimes at least, and this moment felt like a reunion, not a first meeting. Jonah continued, "I have been waiting for this moment your whole life."

Over the next few years, Jonah would become a close friend and now 20 years later is the stream of consciousness that I work with when I am creating programs, channeling group messages, and assisting clients in their spiritual development. Channeling Jonah is like being connected to Source. Accessing my Essence also feels like being connected to Source. I feel the same feelings in my body that I did in church that day when I was 5.

I asked Jonah why he came to me in that way in our first meeting and he replied, "you wanted an experience that would feel safe and lighthearted, so that is what we did. You created the conditions for our meeting." His response has helped me better understand channeling, consciousness, and the nature of our material world. Jonah has guided me and so many others back to ourselves; helping us to feel peace, ease, and trust. My life has become richer and filled with more love and play and prosperity than ever. The more I have trusted my relationship with Jonah, the easier everything has become and the greater the impact I am able to co-create.

Jonah is the messenger behind QUE.

For me to awaken to my Essence I would need to walk through what felt like a trial by fire. I could see that my marriage was coming to an end, and I would need to uproot my entire life, to leave Canada to return to the USA. I was scared and resisted making this change. I would be a single mother again, my business wasn't making enough money to support my lifestyle, and I wasn't in great health. I was still driven to help others to feel better and experience a better life, but I felt like a fraud. The only way forward was trust.

I had studied the Universal Laws, especially the Law of Attraction to better understand how I could improve my conditions and was finding success in waves. I would make money one month and nothing the next. I was writing affirmations, making vision boards, and watching my words like a hawk to ensure my vibration remained high. Unfortunately, my bank account kept dwindling.

On the verge of eviction, fearful about how I would manage, I tried anything I could think of to turn things around. One morning I woke up feeling like it was just too much. I began crying and begging for help from Source, from my guides, from Jonah, from anyone. I felt a desperation that I hadn't felt in 20 years. I felt betrayed by Source. I felt unseen, unheard, and abandoned. I had spent so many years devoted to my growth, caring for others, and being of service to clients. I couldn't understand why I wasn't getting more help and support from the Universe. I felt as though I had gone backwards in my journey.

Was I doing something wrong?

Was I on the wrong track?

Was I unworthy of goodness?

The crying became intense. I was ugly crying – uncontrollably sobbing and shaking with tears covering my face and soaking my clothes. Exhausted from the experience I finally laid down, closed my eyes, and put my hands on my heart. I began repeating a mantra, "I see you, I love you, I am with you."

My mind began to quiet, the tears stopped, and my heart opened.

I began seeing images and hearing instructions through my intuitive senses, which was now a familiar experience. I could feel that Jonah was with me and was eager to share a process with me. I observed everything I was shown and followed the instructions to experience the process. Within moments my body was filled with light and love. It felt like meditation or Reiki but stronger and caused my body to feel activated and filled with energy. I was being filled with Source! My body was buzzing and ready to get up.

I needed to move!

I turned on my favorite music, began dancing around as I opened my laptop. I felt completely reborn and full of trust and belief and enthusiasm for what was next. It was as if I was witnessing my body being moved by Source. I was aware and could feel my body moving and doing things, but I wasn't trying to know what was next, how it would work, or overthinking the idea that was flowing through me. My mind was free. That alone was a miracle, but what followed was magic!

I was inspired to send an email to my clients sharing a new program with them. I was creating the program while I emailed them. The excitement I felt sending the email was so strong that I felt like I had millions in the bank. I didn't care that my account was overdrawn or that I didn't know how I would avoid eviction. I was just excited and eager to live to my fullest! Within 48 hours I went from sobbing tears and no idea how I would move forward to generating enough money to sustain me for an entire year, over 6 figures flooded in within hours. Before this moment I had never made more than $5000 in a month and most months I was barely making a few thousand. This was a shocking experience that felt like a dream.

It wasn't a dream, it was my Essence and I had QUEd up magic.

On the surface, this breakthrough appears to be about money. but it wasn't. What I had discovered was a direct way to tap into the Universal forces that create reality. I had discovered the power for co-creation that has been hidden within us all. I realized that my effort, overwhelm, and struggle were the very things keeping me from what I wanted and instead of fixing my challenges, I needed to select better frequency states.

I was guided to practice the process every day and play with different variations. I began sharing it with some of my closest friends and longtime clients. The results were astounding! What was more astounding is that every day since that day I have received money in some way. I tapped into a force that day that I didn't fully understand, but I was devoted to unlocking it for others. I continued to practice this technique for several years, doubling and tripling my income as I did.

Other things changed too. I began to attract kinder and more loving people into my life. I travel more and experience adventure, more play, and greater wellbeing. This practice isn't just impacting my life, those around me are expanding into more happiness, peace, and ease as well.

My personal experiences with QUE continue to expand. I have come to see myself more clearly and longingly. I have learned to accept myself and express myself fully, as I am, without compromise. I QUE every day.

"Ultimately, I was shown how to tap into the Universe on demand to access the frequencies of my desires."

What is QUE?

QUE stands for Quantum Expansion. Quantum Expansion is a method of isolating and directing the small, quantum, building blocks of reality for the purpose of co-creation. What that means for us is that QUE offers a direct experience with Source, our Essence, and all other frequencies in the Universe. With our mental focus we can direct those frequency waves to become particles in our material experience.

With QUE we access the quantum field and direct frequencies of energy to move through our whole being (Body, Observer, and Essence), to instantly activate our unique biofrequency pattern, and to generate real world results. It is a conscious process that is predictable and repeatable.

What is a biofrequency pattern? Each of us has a unique Frequency that is emitted through the body as light, sound, and geometry, forming a pattern that interacts with all that is to inform and influence reality. Your biofrequency pattern is the combination of all the different frequencies in your YOUniverse. Who you believe you are influences your manifestation ability. When you are operating from a third of your capacity at the level of the physical or emotional body you will emit a distorted pattern. Coming together with your Essence to experience your whole self, as a YOUniverse, is the key to mastering manifestation.

Each biofrequency pattern creates a personal energy signature. Just as your fingerprint and voice are unique to you, so too is your energy field. This is more important to our experience as creators than can be conceived. When we attempt to cover up our true self, we create ripples of distortion throughout our body and the universe is tasked with responding to that distortion with chaos. This can lead to body illness, challenges with loved ones, and physical obstacles of all kinds.

QUE helps you realign with your natural pattern to emit a clear biosignature into the world. This allows you and the Universe to clearly communicate and work together. When you are in dissonance with yourself, you are in dissonance with life itself. You have likely experienced the consequences of this firsthand.

Because your Essence is always in vibrational alignment with the core pattern of who you are, merging it with your Body-Mind and Observer brings instant activation of your YOUniverse. Once your body state changes from a limited physical perception to an aligned multidimensional perception, you can manifest a better experience in the moment. You have the power to pull yourself in and out of these perceptions at will with your Observer-

Mind. It is up to the Observer-Mind to choose alignment with your desire or your disappointment.

You are always free to experience yourself and your life in any way you choose. You can experience a sense of being less than, greater than, or as I AM. If we choose to identify as less than, we identify as a victim of life never having quite enough. If we choose to identify as greater than, we identify as someone who rescues others or the world never having, taking, or giving quite enough. Both of these choices led to disappointment and lack. If we identify as I AM, we unlock wholeness and enoughness that is always adding to and expanding in our experience. We experience the flow of conditions in a natural state of abundance and change.

There is a field of science that helps us understand the impact of inner alignment better called bio-geometry. These scientists study and catalog the biosignatures of humans and other beings by measuring the frequencies emitted in parts of the body, and the body as a whole. These scientists also study the impact of geometry on the body to influence healing outcomes. Measuring the energy emitted by the body, these scientists can witness precise shapes that are formed using highly sensitive frequency devices. The frequency will generate the same shape every time it is measured. The results are predictable and repeatable.

In his book, BioGeometry Signatures: Harmonizing the body's subtle energy exchange with the environment, Dr. Ibrahim Karim (a leading researcher in the field) writes about one of the symbols that has a profound effect on our behavior. Through his research he discovered that the symbol for infinity has an extraordinary effect on the human body. According to Dr. Karim, this symbol "releases the stress caused by past memories" (pg 154, Ibrahim, 2016). Stress is what the body holds in relationship to a belief about the past or present that is out of sync with wellbeing.

Infinity was the symbol I was shown the day I was being taught to use QUE by Jonah and is the foundation for the practice.

I didn't know why each part of the process of QUE was important at the time I was learning it. After 20 years of being guided by Jonah I have come to trust what I am shown in visions, so I practiced the technique without hesitation or doubt. I experimented with the process and found immediate results. I tested those results with more than 100 clients before I discovered Dr. Karim's work with BioGeometry Signatures.

That tearful day, many years ago, Jonah showed me an infinity symbol and directed me to use it as a mental tool for dropping past conditioning and simultaneously bringing the 3 aspects of the multidimensional body into alignment, in the present moment. This simple method makes it possible to activate the energy field of the body in a precise way to intentionally channel universal frequencies. Ultimately, I was shown how to tap into the Universe on demand to access the frequencies of my desires.

Energy & The Law of Proximity

Everything we see, touch, taste and experience is energy that has been organized together at different rates or speeds of movement to create a persistent illusion of liquid, gaseous, or solid states. Frequency is the number of cycles something moves in a pattern of vibration.

Vibration is the movement an object makes in its observed form. Cells move, bodies move, and rocks move but the speed of movement in each cycle is different, which creates a unique manifestation. The frequency pattern is different. The frequency patterns of individual objects within an object (number of cells, organs, fluids, tissues, beliefs, etc.) determine the overall vibration of a person, place, or object. Everything has a unique YOUniverse that they work within to perform their role in the greater Universe.

Every object vibrates.

Every object influences the vibration of other objects.

The closer the objects are, the more that influence is felt in the form of a pattern or frequency of proximity. The further away a vibration is, the less the impact is felt in the frequency pattern. The nearer the vibration is, the more the impact is felt in the frequency pattern. If the vibration of money, for example, is far away, its influence will be minimal on your frequency pattern for wealth. The result may be an experience of wealth that includes other types of objects like bills or debts. If the vibration of money, for example, is nearby, its influence will be more intense on your frequency pattern for wealth. The result may be an experience of gifts, dividends, and payments received.

This is the law of proximity. The closer something is, the more you will experience its presence in your life. To change your overall vibration, you must work with frequency patterns and the law of proximity. To intentionally enhance your vibrational state you can learn, like I did, how to merge with your Essential Self and channel frequency patterns.

Your body has a unique vibration that is first human in its solid body, second emotional in its fluid body, and third spiritual in its gaseous (or spiritual) body. Humans, like water, can experience all 3 states individually or at once. Imagine a Lake that is partially frozen (solid & liquid) that has a low-lying mist (gas) across the top of the water. This theoretical lake is experiencing all 3 conditions at once. For the human these states are experienced through the Body-Mind as a solid semi-fixed state, the Observer-Mind as a temporary fluid state of feeling and sensing, and the Essential Mind as a dream-like, infinite state of intuition and wisdom.

Why is this so important to manifestation? If you don't have the proper biofrequency pattern for what you want the universe will provide an aligned response that seems negative to you. Your biofrequency pattern serves as a coordinate for your location in the Universe – not just where you are physically, but mentally and emotionally too. The Universe uses this feedback for context to provide a matching experience for you and others.

You disrupt your manifestations when you are not aligned with your whole self or YOUniverse.

You disrupt your manifestations when you are not in proximity to the frequency of what you want.

You must be it, to see it. That is, you must be the higher frequency pattern that matches the lower frequency pattern of the material things. Remember the physical things are also more than what you see with your eyes or feel through touch.

You are a YOUniverse within a Universe. The cells of your body are dependent on you being aligned in the proper frequency for well-being, and you are dependent on the Universe being in the proper frequency. When you orient yourself with all of you, the cells in your body sync up, you sync up with the universe, and you activate instant creative powers!

"Happiness is not achieved by having met a goal. Happiness is a frequency you choose as a way of experiencing the journey!"
- Jonah

Taking the "Woo" Out of Manifestation

Just like You, the Universe is made up of the same 3 states of being. The universe is in constant motion and change. The changes are happening in patterns of frequency just like you are experiencing. It's absolute magic to witness it all working together. Trying to sync up with it all can feel like an athlete trying to complete a gauntlet style obstacle course where each decision to stop, to run, or to jump can feel impossible when faced with moving wheels, swinging axes, and falling obstacles. The athletes' timing must be precise to make it through to the goal.

I watched a friend of mine compete in one of the most famous obstacle course events, the Tough Mudder. The course was filled with mud to crawl through, water to swim in, and walls to climb. Seeing her complete the race and still be in one piece was inspiring. Seeing her walk away from the final obstacle to the small table at the finish line to grab her prize, 1 beer, was exhilarating and strangely analogous to many people's lives. I think I spent an entire decade walking through mud and obstacles just to survive and all I got for it was a beer at the end of the week.

You must practice before a gauntlet style obstacle course, especially if there are moving parts. If you aren't prepared, you may have a hard time predicting the frequency intervals for each obstacle. You must be able to regulate your energy, master agility, and have the athletic strength to persevere. Everything in the gauntlet is moving at its own unique pace, never the same as the obstacle before or after it, but if you are observant, there is a pattern that forms. There is a timing to the obstacles that, if you can predict it, you can use to your advantage.

This is the same as the body and the universe. Nothing within you or outside of you is moving at the same pace, creating a seemingly complex web of frequency patterns that you must navigate every moment. It's no wonder humans love control, order and knowing what will come next. No one wants to be bumped out of the game and everyone wants to win.

Therefore, like the gauntlet, it is important to learn the overall pattern of the game – in this case, the game of the Universe. The Universe operates in an overall frequency pattern that Jonah calls the Divine Timing Cycle of Manifestation. Like everything else I have written about so far, the results of working with the Divine Timing Cycle of Manifestation are repeatable and predictable. This cycle is truly life-changing and at the end of each cycle is a lot more than a single beer!

The Divine Timing Cycle of Manifestation is made up of 7 unique stages of thinking, feeling, and doing that are formed by 7 unique frequency patterns. These frequency patterns can be interpreted through mental clues in how you think, emotional clues in how you feel, and physical clues in what is occurring outside of you. When you learn to observe the feedback of these stages, you can quickly discern what stage you are in. You can use your awareness of the pattern to predict what will happen next and use this to your advantage.

You would know when to stop, to run, or to jump like in the gauntlet. You cannot change the order of the cycle or the cycle itself, but you can speed up how fast you move through it. The cycle is fixed, but how you respond is up to you. In the gauntlet you can stand in front of an obstacle if you want, or you can take the leap and move to the next one. In the Divine Timing Cycle, you can sit on a stage as long as you want, or you can take the leap and progress through the cycle to change your experience.

The first step is becoming aware of the cycle itself and then practicing the cycle until you get a feel for it. Once you do, you will be able to run through the cycle and experience manifestation after manifestation after manifestation without breaking a sweat.

Chapter 7

The Divine Timing Cycle of Manifestation

Stage One: Awareness (SEE)

The first step to the Divine Timing Manifestation Cycle is Awareness, when we see (with our inner eye) a new idea, dream, or desire. This stage is primarily experienced in the Body-Mind. During this stage we are thinking about what we like and what we don't like. We are witnessing the conditions in our life and making judgements about them. We may be thinking of new ideas, spending time considering ways we can create a better life for ourselves or others or contemplating what's possible or impossible for us. We want something but we don't yet know how to do, be or have it.

Awareness is the time for setting intentions into motion. It is not the time for justifying how we can achieve our intentions, why we want them, or whether we can have them. This is a time for connecting with the pure potentiality of the universe. This is a great time for journaling, meditating and engaging in conversation to gain new information and perspectives. This is a good time for curiosity and an open mind to help expand our beliefs.

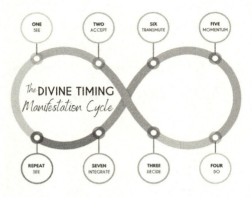

Once you have settled on an intention for yourself – a desire you are ready to pursue further, you will be ready to go from this stage into the next. You will not know how or why or when you will experience your intention. You will only know if you want to explore the possibilities.

Stage Two: Acceptance (ACCEPT)

To be in the stage of Acceptance feels quite different from Awareness. You will notice this stage arises shortly after or during the time when you discover your intention. Your mental state begins to pivot from Body-Mind, as it looks for everything in the way of the intention, to Observer-Mind. You will make a mental belief-inventory as your mind reveals to your Observer-Mind all the beliefs that support the fulfillment of the intention and those beliefs that must be changed to move forward easily.

The key to this stage is recognizing that the seemingly negative belief patterns arising are only here to show you which ones to adjust, not to sabotage you or stop you from pursuing your intention. The key is to witness the beliefs as they arise. They arise first in the mind as a thought:

- I can't do that.
- I don't know how.
- I can't do that because…and so on.

Then, it gets emotional. The emotional aspect of your Body-Mind begins to stir as they respond to the Observer-Mind reorganizing the belief patterns into new, more supportive, patterns.

Each of the old patterns that leave are often experienced as an emotional release, to make room for the new pattern to be formed. This is the stage when you want to witness the process as the Observer-Mind with love for the Body-Mind, helping you to remember that this is a process that is temporary and is in service to your new desire. This may sound tricker than it is. You can use a simple technique I call, "Face It, Feel It, Free It."

Face It, Feel It, Free It allows you to face the old pattern with love and acceptance, welcoming it to rise and be seen and felt. There is no need to understand it, just see and feel the emotion while loving the Body-Mind fully. Like a small child crying because she was ignored by her parents, we need only to invite love and patience with a single thought. We don't need to change the feeling, there is nothing wrong. Once you feel and accept it, you can invite it (with a thought) to move on from this location to experience itself somewhere else.

It's important to understand that the emotions are rising because they are leaving, not because they *need* to leave. There is a big difference. There is nothing wrong and there is nothing you need to do to release it. The release is already happening and your role now is to care for the Body-Mind as it happens, as needed. You have chosen a new experience and these frequency patterns no longer resonate with the new pattern that is forming. That's all, the process is not personal to you or the Universe.

The process of forgiveness can be soothing during this stage, as is shadow work, EFT, Reiki, and other healing modalities that help us recontextualize past experiences. Most useful during this stage is the biogeometric influence of the Infinity symbol. When used as a mental tool for focus it can help collapse old emotional stress and bring your body into the present moment state of wholeness in an instant.

You can try the Face It, Feel It, & Free It and the Instant Forgiveness Techniques on my free downloads page: www.quedownloads.com

Stage Three: Self-Responsibility (DECIDE)

Self-Responsibility is a crucial stage that will determine how, when, and if you proceed to future stages of manifestation. This stage will determine if you will manifest what you intended in the awareness stage. You don't have to clear all your past traumas to manifest, but you do have to get through Self-Acceptance. This stage is about mental and spiritual willingness. Will you decide to have what you want and be willing to do what it takes, to follow your instincts and intuition, and take the steps that lie before you? Will you say yes to what you want no matter what obstacles arise down the path? Will you see this manifestation through to completion?

The key to the Divine Timing Cycle of Manifestation is the trust required to decide to have a thing before you are told how you will do it. Yep, this is the place that has stopped many human beings from having the experiences they want. When we will not let our minds and hearts commit without seeing the physical evidence before the inner evidence, we often give up before even trying. Humans fear disappointment, causing a roadblock. When we demand to know "how" before we say yes, we never say yes. This is because the conditions in our life manifest in the unseen world before the seen world. We say yes within so that we can say yes when it arrives in the physical world later. That's just too uncomfortable for many people. They may fear the risk of embarrassment, failure, and shame more than they desire the bliss of fulfilling new experiences and expanded success.

One of my clients, Allison, recently made the decision to be healthy and well. She committed to it and then amplified her decision using QUE. She shared this with me shortly after:

"I used QUE daily for one week, using the frequency of health and vitality. Within 2 weeks I lost 10 pounds without exercise or dieting and ate whatever I was inspired to eat."

Allison decided what she wanted and that she could have it, then she followed through with the rest of the cycle and she succeeded without effort. If you want to run this gauntlet of manifestation and succeed, you must practice your ability to decide! That means you must decide to believe you can have your intention and that you will take the actions as you are inspired. You must hold that decision firmly in your mind and heart. You must feel the decision and know that it is so. You must be certain that you mean it. You must decide that you will not divorce your intention at the first sign of struggle and you will face whatever challenges arise with love and conviction.

This stage will feel uncomfortable. You will ask how, and you will seek advice and you will attempt to collect evidence to prove you can do what you want to do. You pass this stage when you suspend the need for collecting evidence or defending your dreams, and you decide to **BE THE EVIDENCE** and experience the dream.

You may find yourself defending your limitations in this stage. You may toggle between Acceptance and Self Responsibility, while you adjust patterns and strengthen your self-awareness. Aligning with your Essential Self can bring an instant shift during this stage. When you remember who you are it is easier for your body to believe anything is possible and progress to the next stage.

Stage Four: Activation (DO)

The transition from self-responsibility to activation can feel stark. One minute you are flying high and believing in your dreams and the next you are curled up in a ball crying, wondering why your friends don't support your dreams, or if you are good enough, strong enough, or interesting enough to succeed. Activation opens the door to the first big frequency pattern change that is visible in the outside world. You will begin receiving feedback that your frequency pattern has been shifted by the decision to say Yes in the last stage. The feedback will come in two forms: triggers and synchronicity. Triggers are a nervous system response to conditions that you blame, shame, or judge as wrong. Synchronicities are a nervous system response to conditions that you consider magical or aligned. Both are direct feedback and signs that you are not alone and are being helped by the Divine.

You receive this level of feedback to help you raise your vibration and secure the frequency pattern you just created. The frequency pattern must replicate within all your cells. Those cells that hold old patterns of doubt or disappointment will need to be repatterned. This is an intense stage that is made easier when you practice the Face It, Feel It, Free It technique we mentioned earlier (you can try it here: www.quedownloads.com) and you channel universal frequency patterns, such as love, to support the body's changes.

In this stage there are 3 important signs that indicate it is time to act:

- Synchronicities happen often – time to move forward, don't be complacent

- Triggers happen often – time to move forward, don't look away from what you want
- Doubts, fears, or insecurities come into your awareness – time to pause and love before you do more

This stage will feel a lot like Acceptance felt, with one clear difference. You already said yes to your intention. Reminding yourself what your intention is and recommitting to your yes can help you stay focused.

This stage is often short and results in one of two outcomes:

1. Abandonment of your intention and a return to Awareness. The cycle begins again. This can feel like being pushed off the gauntlet or willingly jumping off for a re-do.
2. Deeper commitment to your intention as you progress to the next stage.

Stage Five: Acceleration (MOMENTUM)

Once you recommit to your intention you will find yourself steadily moving toward your intention. You will be in the "doing" stage, where your dream is being built. This is the stage when most of the progress is happening in a physical way. You are developing the devotion to your intention. This is when you know how you will achieve your dream and you're busy doing it.

Most people enjoy this stage until they get close to the end. In this stage you can feel the progress, and you can see early results. This is the stage that we witness in labor and delivery of a baby when the contractions are steady and it's clear that the baby will arrive soon. This is the stage of plant growth when its flowers are budding, leaves are growing, and the stalks are getting stronger.

As you transition between Activation into Acceleration you will notice 3 key characteristics:

- You may wonder, "When will it happen?"
- You may complain, "I'm too tired - I don't think I can wait any longer."
- You may worry, "Why hasn't it happened yet."

This is the time when channeling frequency from the Universe can give the extra energy needed to break through. Caring for yourself and nurturing your intentions are critical. Your attention to detail now will make all the difference in the quality of the outcome.

Stage Six: Transmutation (TRANSMUTE)

As you reach the final moments, hours, or days of a manifestation cycle you will enter the stage of Transmutation. This stage is often surprisingly quiet and relieving. Transmutation is the experience of becoming. One moment you feel one way and the next you are changed. You cannot always recognize what has changed, but it is inarguable that you have. As an example, becoming a parent for the first time. There is an obvious change in the arrival of a new human; however, there is a less obvious change in the way you perceive life and yourself. The changes may not be fully understood for a while, perhaps even years. Another example would be moving homes. The physical home changes right away, but the emotional, mental, and social changes that happen within may not be evident for a while.

To master this stage is important. At the completion of a journey you are being prepared for the next one. Humans are creators. They will be pulled by the energy around them to continue to contribute to the unfolding of the trillions of simultaneous manifestation cycles. When you focus your attention on transmutation you will be conscious of selecting a new intention. If you do not select a new intention, the world around you will begin to pull you into the strongest intentions around you. This can create drama, trauma, and frustration.

What to be aware of during Transmutation:

Celebrate on your own or with others when you reach a goal, dream, or intention of any size. This helps you acknowledge the end of a cycle consciously and release any identification you have with who you were before so that you can honor who you are today.

Integrate the changes with love by reflecting on the journey and offering gratitude to yourself and those who supported you along the way. This helps to amplify the energy of belonging, abundance, and love for the next cycle.

Stage Seven: The In-Between (INTEGRATE)

This is the stage when you are being present with your life - as it is. When you observe what has changed physically you will begin to witness how your perception of the outside world has changed too. Take time during this cycle to notice the habits you have in place and to practice presence. Do not see things as you were, but as you are. Greet life with the eyes of a curious child. Ask questions about what things mean to you now. Allow your Mind-Body to synchronize with your new conditions.

Evaluate the experience you are having with your life now and choose the elements you love and want more of. Are there any new things you want to experience now that you hadn't thought about before? This will help you direct the thought energy that arrives next as you enter the next cycle.

This time will be a brief pause from the obstacle course. You will know it is over when you begin to feel the pull to make changes or experience more. That is when the active stage of Awareness begins again.

Chapter 8

The Universe is Neutral

Using QUE consciously during these stages helps to bring frequencies into closer proximity to you at key times in the Manifestation Cycle. The reason this is so powerful is that it will give you a boost of energy that you can leverage to accelerate the accomplishment of any desire, goal, or intention. Not only will QUE help accelerate your progress, but it will also help you love the journey!

"Happiness is not achieved by having met a goal. Happiness is a frequency you choose as a way of experiencing the journey!" - Jonah

The Universe is neutral which means the stages of the Divine Timing Manifestation Cycle are also neutral. The cycle wants nothing from you, nor does it judge what's good or bad to create. The cycle is simply operated by Universal law, weaving the frequencies together to generate the tapestry of life. The Manifestation Cycle is like the spider and its silk, moving from point to point to build the web, in this case, the web of life. In this analogy, you guide the spider's movements with your frequencies as she animates the web into form. She is guided by an inspiration to move from tree trunk to rock to grass. She is not considering how long the web will survive because she knows that she can easily build another. She seeks the best place in the moment by trusting the strongest impulses. She cannot know if the wind will come and wipe her web out. She cannot know when the insect will make its way to the web. She simply does what is inspired and waits for the feedback before she responds – a tug on the small fiber of the web.

The spider has a superpower of hypersensitivity to movement (aka frequency). When something outside of herself interacts with the web a subtle frequency travels along a path of silken thread and she follows it to the source to see what has arrived for her. You have this superpower too, but the threads that you feel are invisible to you, as the frequencies travel in non-visible circuits of light between your heart and the Quantum Field.

Just like all spiders can sense the frequency that travels through their web, all humans can sense the frequency that travels through the quantum field of their Essential Body. You can sense the presence of other people and things by the frequency they emit as they come closer to you. Practicing QUE helps you to develop your use of this superpower to not only sense what's arriving but to send information into the field to draw specific types of people and objects closer. Humans are equipped with the ability to build a quantum field around themselves but also have an additional superpower – a type of telecommunication and electromagnetism in one.

Each Divine Timing Manifestation Cycle is either a new quantum field or a reinforcement of your current field. You are either creating a new story or remodeling the old one – a new web or enhancing the existing web. Transmutation is when you can test the field you have built, and The In-between is when you wait for the feedback before you can proceed. Based on how you feel about the feedback you will maintain your current experience, or you build something new and a new Divine Timing Manifestation Cycle begins.

In the beginning of your journey with QUE much of your inspiration to create will be based on something you feel is missing from your life or something that feels broken, incomplete, or unfulfilled. You may find yourself doing this as you learn to release any lack-based thinking. Over time you will experience the contentment of knowing who you are, that you are abundant, and connected to all that you desire. You will feel whole and complete with all that you are and what you experience. This is when life can open doors for you! This is when what you create is for the pure joy of creation and you will get a greater sense of what it is like to be a co-creator in this 3rd dimension. You will no longer see life through the lens of what you should create but instead what you choose to create!

As a conscious creator, I now wake up every morning with the same routine:

1. I express my love and gratitude for life!
2. I QUE to release the past and acknowledge the present moment.
3. I ask myself, what would be fun to create today?

4. I QUE the frequencies of whatever arises in response to the question.

By focusing on what is fun to create, rather than what I need, I automatically access all that I need throughout the day. I tap into the highest core frequency of what I want and everything that is required for the experience to unfold, unfolds.

Another client shared her story about using QUE at a recent sporting event.

My son Wyatt and I went to the Iowa Basketball game tonight.

Iowa played against the Indiana Hoosiers. Iowa was 0-4 going into this game, and Indiana was slated to win the Big 10 division. We basically had no shot.

We were down by 20 pts within 5 minutes.

But then something happened.

Something started to shift.

I know my personal vibration is very high. I measure it and work with it every day doing QUE. I know that my son has a very high vibration and I could feel the two of us emanating our frequency out toward the basketball court. I noticed the crowd around us starting to shift. People started to act more positively. The crowd became more enthusiastic and the team was responding.

I kept saying to Wy, wouldn't it be fun if we won?

And we did!! By 1 point!!

It was indeed so fun.

Because life is fun.

And win or lose we had fun.

The next day, I posted this on FB with my photos and a woman who I know reached out and said that she was at the game, at the exact moment that the momentum of the game shifted, she said she could feel it too and noticed throughout the entire game how the vibration of the crowd had completely shifted. It was such a tangible and physical manifestation coming through and a total blast to witness! —Jennifer Kohler

Practicing QUE does not give us power over others, or over a basketball game. What it does do is give us immense power to love the experience no matter what and to be a positive influence to the people around us.

"You cannot buy your way to wholeness; it is something you must cultivate within you."

The Essential FreQUEncies

Chapter 9

The Essential FreQUEncies

Merging with your Essence can alleviate all suffering for the Body-Mind. There is nothing more powerful or essential to the well-being, happiness, and success of an individual than the relationship they have with themselves, with a clear connection to their Essence. Money, relationships, successful careers, and good friendships are wonderful, but they do not give to the individual what the Essence can, the Essential Frequencies of Life.

The Essential FreQUEncies:

- Love
- Belonging
- Acceptance
- Value
- Trust
- Freedom
- Creator
- Source

The Essential Frequencies will bring money, people, and things into your life experience, but money, people, and things will not bring the Essential Frequencies. You cannot buy your way to wholeness; it is something you must cultivate within you. So, even if you have money, relationships, or career opportunities you will still feel unfulfilled in these areas of your life until you cultivate the frequency within your own Body-Mind. This is wholeness.

Cultivating wholeness is a process of collapsing the illusions and distortions you have created under the belief patterns of separation you developed by not knowing your Essence. Everyone is born a whole being with all 3 body levels connected and guiding them. Over time, this connection is distorted by belief patterns related to needs. This physical body, unable to care for itself, must trust the world to nurture them and keep them alive. As you know, childhood comes with a lot of confusing experiences, emotional challenges, and sometimes physical trauma. By the time you are 7 years old you have forgotten your Essence and fully identify with the world as your source of supply for the Essential Frequencies of life.

The physical world can never provide you the Essential Frequencies, at least not for long. Physical energy can only be borrowed for a time. The only infinite energy available is from the unseen, quantum world. That doesn't stop people from attempting to get their needs met by borrowing the energy of others. The tragic result is the development of mental illusions that keep each person from wholeness. The longer a person reaches for their wholeness in another, the more severe the pain and suffering becomes. Fleeting moments of happiness keep people trying, or surrendering to a belief that life is hard, not fair, or cruel. People attempt to outrun their challenges by chasing shiny objects and promises of quick success, pleasure, and happiness. It is no surprise to me that mental health issues are steadily escalating.

When you merge all three body levels and learn to think from the higher perspective of the Essence you begin to experience the world as an abundant and playful place. The merging process will cause your thoughts, emotions, and behavior patterns to shift. You will notice that what you once needed becomes available to you instantly.

Where you may have felt abandoned or left behind due to rejection or loss in the past, you will now experience love, belonging, and connection. Neglect and lack become abundance and flow. Abuse and violence become kindness and love. Betrayal and hatred become trust and adoration. Boredom and debt become adventure and freedom. Deceit and illusion become truth and knowing. These are not emotions, but frequencies that are innate to your Essence that trigger emotional and physical responses of wholeness. Because the Essence adheres to the Universal Laws in its thinking, it cannot conceive of being separate from these states of being. Imagine what this might feel like right now, to have all needs met within. Imagine feeling wholeness, fulfillment, and peace.

Advanced manifesting is not about making a list of things you want from the Universe like a shopping list. Advanced manifesting is about living in a state of abundance that is always expanding in accordance with

Universal Law. Experiences that you love are always flowing to and through you. You learn to be precise with frequency, not details of the things. Advanced manifesting turns the tap on to a direct connection with the Universe. Your job is to stay connected by merging with your Essence.

Chapter 10

YOUniversal Awakening

When we merge with our Essence and begin living consciously as a YOUniverse we can still be tempted to forget who we are. The world around us reminds us that most people do not remember who they are. Being an advanced manifestor is not common, yet. As we expand our awareness, we will expand our trust as well. Your YOUniverse operates on faith in Source. There are some things that you will never have answers to. The unknown is what triggers us back into our lowest vibrational self, the Body-Mind.

Most of the time the Observer can offer support for this unknown experience. The Observer can offer reassurance that we will be safe, we are loved, or all is well. This reassurance will take practice in the beginning. Remember, the Body-Mind only wants to keep the body safe, and it must find a way to survive or surrender to its death. This is the only way that the Body-Mind can move forward without breaking down and the Observer learns to support this aspect of the self with inner dialogue – patterns of thought. However, when the Observer cannot or does not reassure the Body-Mind, there is a breakdown that occurs that lets fear rise up to ensure survival. When we are in survival-mode, we do not create abundance, we create protection.

This is one of the core reasons we don't experience consistent manifestation and, instead, experience a wide pendulum swing between good and bad outcomes. The Observer is the steward of healing. Once healing is complete, the conditions in life take on a new meaning. Life is now ready to be seen from an expanded perception where play and exploration is the dominant creative impulse. It is time to see beyond fixing and healing.

This shift in perception and experience is guided by the Essence. First, we must understand what takes place during these awakenings. When we notice more unknown things in our lives, it is a sign we are awakening. We are awakening to new perceptions. In the Body-Mind we learn to be more aware of ways to meet survival needs. We access greater intelligence. We eventually max out our potential in this 3-dimensional experience. We begin to become aware of the shortcomings. We begin to seek deeper meaning beyond money and things and achievement. We awaken to the Observer. This is what happened to me when I was meditating and discovering Reiki.

We then go through the merging process of the Body-Mind with the Observer, and we feel the euphoria of awakening. We access greater truths of how the Body-Mind works and we journey into healing. We discover ways to direct our thoughts to meet our need for meaning. We eventually max out our potential in this 4th

dimensional experience. So again, we feel the unknown as we awaken to our Essence in the 5th dimension. We awaken to new perceptions of unity and something beyond healing and meaning making. We awaken to a creative process that we seek to understand and master. Yet, the Observer has no way of mastering this alchemy without fully merging with the Essence. This is what happened to me when I awakened through QUE.

What stage of awakening do you find yourself in as you read this book?

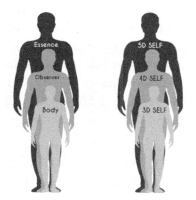

5D - Unity Consciousness
4D - Emotional Consciousness
3D - Physical Consciousness

When I was shown the process of QUE I was at the doorway to a shift in consciousness from identifying with my Observer to merging with my Essence. It began the moment I decided to stop healing, triggering an emotional roller coaster like never before. I was mastering my thoughts, regulating my emotions, meditating and doing all of the things that had brought me amazing physical results before. I found myself burning out to keep up with building my dreams. I knew my Essence was available to me, but I didn't know how to let her all the way in. I didn't even know what that meant. I just kept asking her and Jonah to help me. They kept guiding, but I became exhausted by having to remember to ask and making space to connect with my Essence. I was missing something.

I look back at this time in my life and now see that it was a grieving of my identity as a spiritual human. The answer was right in front of me, but I never asked the right question. I didn't ask the right question because I wasn't ready to give up the identity I had created. I wanted to stop healing, but I didn't want to give "me" up. I thought I would have to give up being human when I merged with my Essence. I had always seen others who had awakened to this state of being as somehow less human. They were like Gods to me. People had worshiped these people throughout history. Who was I to awaken to this level? Could I really do it? Should I really do it? Would I lose all my friends, my family, my career?

The pull of my purpose was bigger than my fear of losing my identity or of death. When I connected with my Essence, I would remember who I was and why I was here on Earth. The more I connected with her, the more I would remember and the stronger the pull became. It became painful in the Body-Mind to ignore the truth of my whole self. The Body-Mind and the Observer found more meaning in awakening than surviving and over time I was able to surrender. My Body-Mind needed to know what happened on the other side of the awakening more than it needed to hold on. The Observer was willing, and she helped bring peace and ease to the Body-Mind.

We are all headed toward this awakening. The enlightened ones from our stories were ahead of their time. They were paving the way for us. They were the lighthouses guiding our path. Their stories and teachings help us remember now. They continue to work with us long after their deaths through ancient texts and teachings, religious ministries, and through spiritual channels.

They are helping you right now. They are available to you right now. Jonah was my guide through this process. With the love and support of Jonah, it was easier for me to trust the process of surrendering and merging with my Essence. I finally asked the right question, "What is the next best step to experience what I want?"

"Advanced manifesting is about living in a state of abundance that is always expanding in accordance with Universal Law."

Advanced Manifestation

Order is everything. The order of how we do anything is the key to our ease, peace, and enjoyment of everything. If you pack your bags and get into the car but you don't know where you are going, you won't go far. If you want a successful career, but you don't pick a field to study, you will never feel fulfilled. If you want a better relationship, but you don't know what a better relationship is…I think you see the point. Order is everything and awareness of what you want is the first step.

Advanced Manifestation with QUE is easy, predictable, and repeatable. All you need to do is say yes to being your whole self and begin the advanced manifestation journey.

1. The first step is to merge with your Essence and instantly activate your YOUniverse. This process takes activation and practice. Jonah took

me through a 90-day process of merging with my Essence before I was shown the rest of the process of manifestation. The time it takes is different for everyone. I have found that most people integrate their Essence in about 30 days of consistent practice.

2. The second step is learning to integrate the Essential Frequencies and practice amplifying them with others intentionally.
3. The third step is to learn to work with the manifestation cycle precisely to direct frequency throughout the 7 stages of Divine Timing.
4. The fourth step is sharing QUE with others as a certified Advanced Manifestation Mentor if you feel inspired. To teach is when we learn the most. As an Advanced Manifestation Mentor, you learn the Universal Laws that support the process as well as how to support others in the Activation of their Essence and the manifestation cycle.

If you are ready to activate your Essence and unlock the magical world of Advanced Manifestation with QUE join the 30-Day Essence Activation - Free at www.que30.com.

Chapter 11

Taking the Leap

The thoughts we think are a result of the awareness and integration of the 3 minds within the physical body. Meditation, yoga, and mindfulness are popular tools for awakening to the Observer and the Essence. However, without guidance, this can open people up to confusion around how to apply what they discover. As a result, many who have awakened find themselves more in their bodies than before, attempting to control the conditions they experience, habitually healing and traumatizing the physical body for health, wealth, or physical pleasure. Many find themselves chasing new awakening experiences and energetic highs that distract them from the deeper truths and experiences available.

Some find themselves escaping the body to experience the higher planes by spending more time out of the physical body than in it. This can lead to feeling ungrounded and ineffective at living their lives with ease, peace, and prosperity without considerable effort or mental distortion. Many find themselves wanting to leave the body for the next life and struggle to accept conditions as they are. Worse still, they find it challenging to manifest solutions that are lasting or consistent. Everything that worked before now falls short.

The eventuality of this confusion is a general dissatisfaction with life and disillusionment with the spiritual journey. They find themselves living in extreme highs and lows or mediocre experiences to avoid disappointment. For some, this will lead to bitterness and an abandonment of their higher self, never discovering there is more for them in this life. For others, the seekers, their confusion will fuel curiosity, offering a doorway into deeper discovery and connection with their Essence, who will begin to point them to the truth of who they are.

When you are aware of these 3 body levels and develop a connection with them intentionally, you gain access to the whole self and activate immense power that appears supernatural or mystical to others. Life begins to fall into place, conditions improve rapidly, and satisfaction is fulfilled. However, it's not magic. Everything I am sharing with you in this book is accessible to all people who are open, curious, and willing to give QUE a try.

However, there is a third group of people who have not yet had an awakening experience of any kind. These are people who find themselves in a state of constant survival with little or no time for themselves. They are working multiple jobs, facing financial hardship, caring for young kids or aging parents, or frightened by the headlines and feeling hopeless or lost. The idea that there is an Essential Self that could help them escape these conditions is enticing but they are simply too exhausted to give it a try. They just don't realize that QUE is so easy to learn and simple to practice in just a few minutes each day. They consider spirituality a luxury they can't yet afford. These individuals will be nudged by their Essence soon – through a body illness, personal loss, or trauma that leads them to a healer, coach, or lightworker who sits with them and guides them through a simple energy practice called QUE. Maybe that person will be you. My mission is, with your help, to share QUE with as many people as possible. The time for a radical leap in wellbeing is now.

If you have gotten this far, you have already begun the process. You are already remembering that you are whole and there is more to who you are than your body. You are already awakening to higher frequencies and well on your way to being an Advanced Manifestor. All that is left is for you to take the Leap.

About the Author

Moving from corporate executive to spiritual mentor, Joy Kingsborough has leveraged her diverse background in leadership, coaching, healing, and her love of quantum physics with her business and psychology degrees to inspire her audiences and students to connect more deeply with themselves and the Divine.

Her popularity has risen among wisdom seekers, coaches, and healers due to her simple, non-dogmatic, and scientifically inspired approach to awakening to higher consciousness. She has been a channel for more than 20 years, is an expert in meditation and mindfulness, and is the creator of Quantum Expansion (aka QUE).

Joy's journey has been an inside-out experience of personal, professional, and spiritual inquiry that has led to her devotion to be of service to the awakening journey of others. She is passionate about sharing the magic of the Universe in a way that is light-hearted and simple.

Are You Looking For A Speaker?

Are you looking for a speaker for your event? Joy travels the world to speak on stages and inspire audiences to trust their intuition, activate their purpose, and become an advanced manifestor.

Book Joy to speak or lead a workshop at your next event, workshop, or retreat: www.advancedmanifestor.com

Made in the USA
Las Vegas, NV
03 March 2024

86672105R00059